Contents

Introduction

The collections of the Metropolitan Museum of Art encompass over three million objects, including some of the greatest works of art in the world. Some are thousands of years old; others were made as recently as this year. There are paintings, sculptures, tapestries, precious jewelry, ceramics, prints, entire rooms from houses, and even an Egyptian temple!

The museum also houses objects that were used by people throughout history in their everyday lives, such as clothing, fans, clocks, tableware, weather vanes, musical instruments, religious objects, games, and furniture. They show us that the most practical and ordinary objects in our lives can be great works of art when they are made with imagination and care.

Many of these objects can be seen in the galleries of the museum. But even though the museum is very large—over 1.4 million square feet—there is unfortunately not enough space to display everything. Behind the walls of exhibitions and in attics, basements, and tunnels are temperature-controlled storage rooms that house books, prints, and works of art that are displayed from time to time and that travel to other museums.

Part of my job at the museum is to have the works of art (on view and in storage) photographed and printed on postcards, posters, and in books so that people can learn about them and study them. Over the years I came across games and toys in the collection and began to wonder just how many "amusements" there were. Last year I decided to find as many of them as I could and set out on a treasure hunt through the museum. I searched the galleries and storage room shelves and boxes and read many publications, some from as far back as the 1600s. I found old photographs and descriptions in files and traced them back to the objects, which were safely stored away. And what a treasure hunt! I discovered puzzles, board games, puppets, paper dolls, paper theaters, advertising cards, kites, and toys made by civilizations ancient to modern.

Now it is your turn to go on a treasure hunt. I have tried to make this book into a small museum filled with some of the objects I found in the Metropolitan. You can wander through these pages at your leisure as though they were galleries and storage rooms. Rediscover some of the museum's many treasures, creations of a wealth of civilizations. Take them and make them your own.

—Osa Brown

How to Use This Book

This book is filled with models, toys, and games. Before you start an activity, read the directions through from beginning to end. Think of the models as guides to show you how the objects are made, and then invent your own creations. Make ancient designs and designs of the future. Create the zaniest mask you can think of, the funniest zoetrope movies possible, the most beautiful kite you can. Let your imagination soar!

Gather all the tools and materials you will need for an activity. If you must substitute one material for another or spend time finding tools, do it before you begin.

For the projects that need cutting, pasting, and coloring, decide first where you will work. You should get your parents' approval for the best place. Spread newspapers over the surface you will work on and wear old clothes or an old, large shirt over your clothes. (Felt-tip markers, paste, and paint can stain clothing.)

If you have to stop working on a project before you have completed it, gather your materials and store them where you can easily reach them again. Remember to replace all lids on containers, wash brushes, and throw away the newspapers. When the project is finished, put all the tools back where they belong. You might want to save leftover materials for your next project.

Here are the basic craft techniques you will need to make the projects.

Taping:

It is important to use transparent tape that has a dull surface so you can write over it with pencils, pens, crayons, or paints.

To tape together two pieces of paper, as in the Mansion of Happiness board game (pp. 6 and 7), lay the two pieces side by side, the way they will be when they are attached.

Cut a piece of tape a little longer than the side to be taped.

Hold the tape over the edge where the two pieces of paper meet so that half the tape is over one side, half is over the other, and there is a bit of tape hanging over each end, as shown.

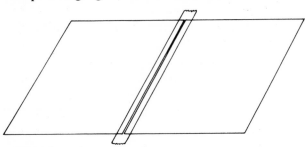

Press and rub the tape down onto the paper. Fold the two ends around the back.

Turn the paper over and do the same to the other side.

For the board games, the weather vane, and the mosaic you will need to seal the paper to the cardboard after they have been glued together.

To do this, cut a piece of tape a little longer than one side of the object to be taped. Turn the paper and cardboard so the paper is on top.

Hold the tape above one edge of the paper so that half the tape is over the paper, half extends over the edge, and a bit of tape hangs over each end, as shown. Press the tape down on the paper, letting the rest stick straight out. Cut off the two ends. Wrap the rest of the tape around the cardboard.

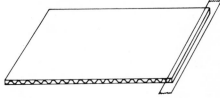

Turn the cardboard side up and do the same on that side.

Tape each edge in the same way. This will keep the edges of the paper from curling.

There are two ways of gluing paper and cardboard together with rubber cement.

Wet mounting:

Apply glue to the surface of one of the two pieces of paper or cardboard you are joining together. Let dry.

Apply glue to the surface of the other piece and, while it is still wet, line up the edges of both pieces (the two glued sides facing each other) and press both surfaces together.

Dry mounting:

Do this slowly and carefully—once two papers are dry mounted together, they will not come apart. This is harder to do than wet mounting, but it is the strongest way of gluing paper together. You can also dry mount paper to cardboard, as in the Weather Vane (p. 24). When dry mounting, besides the glue and paper, you will need two other pieces of very light paper (tracing, tissue, onion skin, or looseleaf paper) that are larger than the two pieces you are gluing together.

Apply glue to the surface of one of the two pieces of paper you are joining together. Let dry.

Apply glue to the surface of the other piece and let it dry also.

Place the first piece glued side up. Put the two pieces of tracing paper over it, one on the right

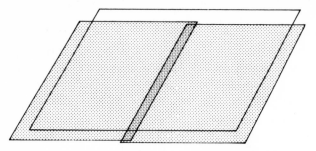

and one on the left. Have the pieces of tracing paper overlap slightly down the middle. Allow about ⅟₁₆ inch of the glued paper to stick out on top. The tracing paper will not stick to the dried glue.

Place the second piece of paper, glued side face down, on top of the tracing paper, *making sure to line up the top edges of both glued sheets*. Now check that all the edges of both glued sheets match.

Holding down the left side of the top sheet, gently pull out the piece of tracing paper on the right until it extends about 2 inches on the right. Press down the middle of the top glued sheet, to make the two glued papers stick together. Slide out the whole right piece of tracing paper, and press down on the right side of the top glued paper.

Holding down the right side of sheet, gently slide out the left piece of tracing paper. Press down the left side of the glued paper. The two papers are now bonded together.

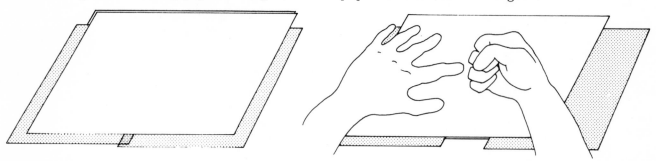

Enlarging:

This is a way of copying a picture from a book onto a sheet of paper and making it any size you want it to be. The Carp Kite (p. 15) is the only activity that calls for this method, but you can enlarge anything in the book or any picture in any book or magazine.

Note that a 1-inch-square grid has already been drawn over the carp banner. On a large piece of paper, draw a grid made of squares 3 inches by 3 inches. Number the boxes in pencil as they are numbered on page 16.

Copy the part of the outline of the carp that is in square #1 in the book onto square #1 of the grid you have drawn.

Copy the outline that is in square #2 in the book onto square #2 of your grid. Do the same for every square. Copy the outline of the carp from all the boxes in the book onto your grid, one by one, left to right, line by line.

Using this method, you can copy and enlarge the whole body design of the carp onto your grid

as well. This takes a lot of care and patience and may take a long time, so you might want to draw your own design inside the carp outline instead.

Now it's time to begin. You have hours of excitement ahead of you. Just turn the page and enter the world of the Metropolitan Museum of Art.

The Fan

A million years ago a prehistoric being may have pulled a leaf off a tree and waved it to keep cool—inventing the fan. Ramses the Great, the Egyptian pharaoh who ruled in 1300 B.C.E. (Before the Common Era), gave only his most trusted men the privilege of holding his fans for him. The ancient Egyptians, Assyrians, Chinese, Japanese, and Greeks used fans in religious ceremonies and as symbols of power. The women of France, Spain, and Italy wore fans with every outfit and used them to flirt with.

Folding and rigid fans have always been especially important in Japan. They are used by warriors, actors, children, emperors, and heads of state. They are given as presents and serve as trays for holding gifts. And in Japan the fan has a very special meaning: the top of the handle symbolizes the beginning of life, and the ribs of the fan stand for the roads of life spreading out in all directions toward a future filled with good fortune.

A woodcut by Kitao Masanobu, a Japanese artist who lived from 1761 to 1816.

You will need:

19 Popsicle sticks—you can buy these in packages at crafts stores, so you don't have to eat 19 Popsicles!

permanent felt-tip markers, crayons, tempera paints, or watercolors

scissors
pencil
stiff paper
ruler
glue
masking tape

What to do:

1. Cut out fan-front along outline.

2. Trace around fan-front on paper and cut out shape. This will be the back of the fan, for you to decorate.

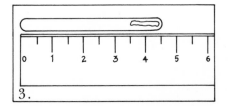

3. Lay a Popsicle stick next to the ruler so that one end lines up with zero. Put about an inch of glue on the other end of the stick as shown.

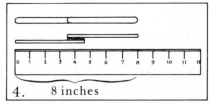

8 inches

4. Place a second stick over the first so the 2 sticks together become 8 inches long. Press the sticks together. This is one "rib" for the fan.

5. Glue 2 more sticks together to make another rib. Then repeat. You now have 3 ribs.

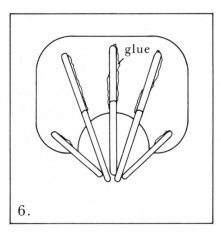

6.

6. Turn the fan-front face down. Glue the 3 ribs as shown. Then glue a single Popsicle stick to each corner as shown.

7. Put glue all over the back of the fan-front and the sticks. Carefully place fan-back over fan-front, matching up the edges. Press firmly.

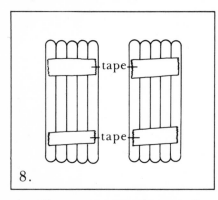

tape

tape

8.

8. Place 5 Popsicle sticks on a flat surface, side by side. Put a strip of masking tape along the top and bottom.

Do the same with 5 more sticks. Each group of sticks will be half the handle of the fan.

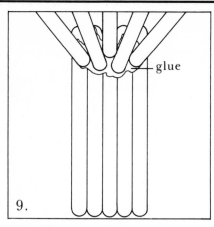

glue

9.

9. Turn one half of the fan handle over so the masking tape is on the bottom. Spread glue on the top inch or so. Then press the ends of the fan ribs into the glue as shown.

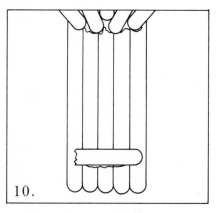

10.

10. Break a small piece (less than 2 inches) off the last Popsicle stick and glue across handle as shown. Press down and let dry.

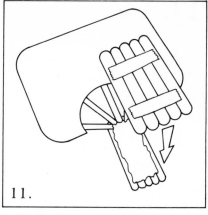

11.

11. Put glue all over the handle half to which you've just attached the stick piece. Making sure masking tape is on top, press down other half of handle onto the half with the glue as shown. Let dry.

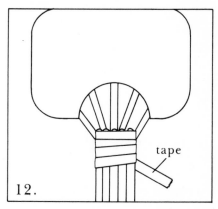

tape

12.

12. Wrap the masking tape around handle from top to bottom.

13. Color handle with marker and your fan is finished.

Using this method, you can make a fan in the shape of a circle, square, rectangle, or any other shape. Fans have been made of branches and ostrich and peacock feathers, and have been decorated with pearls and diamonds. Decorate your fan with feathers, cloth, sea shells, sequins, glitter, or colored paper. For a fan with a longer handle, use sticks glued end to end like ribs. Make a floppy fan with long pipe cleaners for ribs.

And on the next hot summer day you can use your energy-saving fan to keep cool!

3

TEETOTUM

4

The Mansion of Happiness

At this amusement each will find
A moral fit t'improve the mind:
It gives to those their proper due,
Who various paths of vice pursue,
And shows (while vice destruction brings)
That good from every virtue springs.
Be virtuous then and forward press,
To gain the seat of happiness.

—from Mansion of Happiness
game board, 1843

Did you know there were board games more than 3,000 years ago? Spiral board games have been popular since ancient Egyptian times. The Mansion of Happiness is a printed spiral board game that was played in America in the 1800s. The game taught children what was good behavior and what was bad. Good children were grateful and honest. In the game players landing on the squares marked Gratitude and Honesty moved more quickly to the goal—the Mansion of Happiness. Bad children were cruel and boastful. So players landing on the squares marked Cruelty and Audacity lost a turn. Drunks were put in the stocks, and so on.

You will need:

scissors
toothpick
light cardboard

transparent tape
rubber cement or white
glue

a different color or shape marker for each player. You can use buttons, coins, pebbles, markers from other games, and so on.

What to do:

1. Cut out teetotum (page 4).

2. Punch a hole in the center of teetotum with the toothpick. Remove toothpick.

3. Trace teetotum on cardboard and cut out. Glue or dry mount (see p. vii) teetotum to cardboard.

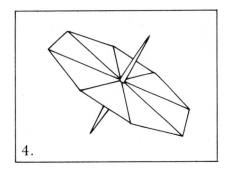
4.

4. Push toothpick halfway through teetotum. Now it can spin like a top.

5. Cut game board out along outline. Tape the 2 pieces of the game together side by side. Be sure to save the rules for playing—you'll need them later. Trace the game board onto a piece of cardboard, then cut out the rectangle. Glue or dry mount game board, colored side up, to cardboard, press down, and let dry.

Tape edges of paper onto cardboard (see p. vii).

Now you are ready to play the Mansion of Happiness.

A teetotum (tee-TOE-tum) is a small top that is used in games instead of dice. When it is spun, the number that lands on the uppermost side tells you how many spaces you can move. See page 4.

How to play:

Any number can play. All the players take turns spinning the teetotum. The one who gets the highest number on its topmost section goes first. The player to his right goes next, and so on. Each player spins the teetotum in turn and moves his counter the number of squares it shows. Whoever arrives first at #67, the MANSION OF HAPPINESS, wins.

If a player happens to land on POVERTY, the WHIPPING POST, the HOUSE OF CORRECTION, the PILLORY, the STOCKS, PRISON, or RUIN on his way to the MANSION, he may leave on his next turn.

When a second player lands on an already occupied square, the first player must go back to where the second player came from. But when a second player lands by chance on the HOUSE OF CORRECTION or PRISON and it is already full, the second player must go back where he came from and spin again. If the second player is *sent* to the HOUSE OF CORRECTION or PRISON, then the first player is free to move on his next turn.

If you land on #6, the WATER, go to #10.

If you arrive at #9, the INN, go to #12.

Whoever lands on PIETY, HONESTY, TEMPERANCE, GRATITUDE, PRUDENCE, TRUTH, CHASTITY, SINCERITY, HUMILITY, INDUSTRY, CHARITY, HUMANITY, or GENEROSITY can move ahead 6 more squares toward the MANSION OF HAPPINESS.

Whoever lands on AUDACITY, CRUELTY, IMMODESTY, or INGRATITUDE must go back where he came from until his next turn.

Whoever lands on PASSION must be taken to the WATER for a ducking to cool him off.

Whoever lands on IDLENESS must go to POVERTY.

Whoever lands on the ROAD TO FOLLY must return to PRUDENCE.

Whoever becomes a SABBATH BREAKER must be taken to the WHIPPING POST and whipped.

Whoever becomes a CHEAT must go to the HOUSE OF CORRECTION and miss his turn.

Whoever is a PERJURER must go to the PILLORY.

Whoever is a DRUNKARD must be put in the STOCKS.

Whoever becomes a ROBBER must be sent to PRISON and lose his next 2 turns.

And whoever arrives at the SUMMIT OF DISSIPATION *must* go to RUIN.

Whoever arrives first at the MANSION OF HAPPINESS wins the game; but you must spin the exact number of squares to reach it. If you throw over the right number, return to the SEAT OF EXPECTATION and spin again in turn until you spin the exact number that will take you to the MANSION OF HAPPINESS.

6

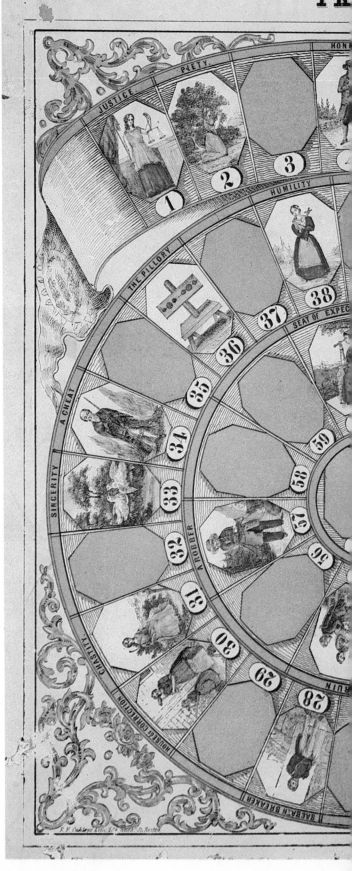

MANSION OF HAPPINESS.

AN INSTRUCTIVE MORAL AND ENTERTAINING AMUSEMENT.

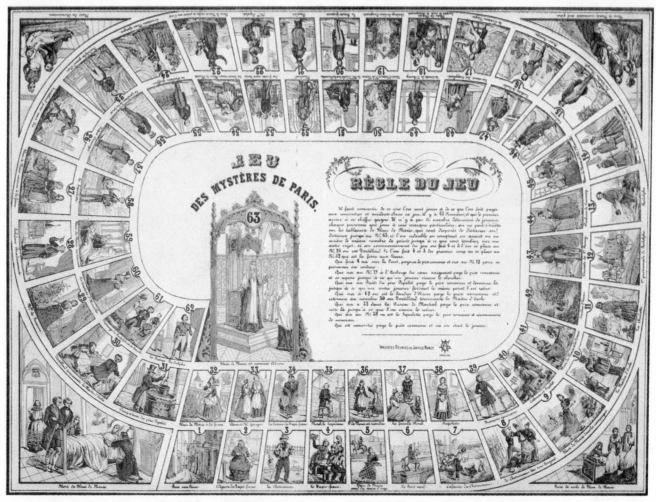

The Mysteries of Paris, a French spiral board game from 1850 that was based on the Game of Goose.

The Mansion of Happiness was based on an Italian game called the Game of Goose. The Game of Goose was played in the 1500s by kings and noblemen. Soon it spread throughout Europe and at last to America.

This Goose game board was made in northern Italy between 1500 and 1540. It is teakwood inlaid with other woods, ivory, and stone. On the reverse side of this board is an inlaid chess board.

Pantins

Jumping dolls go back more than 2,000 years. This type of jumping doll was first made in the town of Pantin (pan-TAN), France, over 200 years ago. Pantins—named after the town—were children's toys at first, but soon everyone was charmed by them. The people of France played with them in the streets and entertained guests with Pantins in their homes. A rich man lost his fortune because he hired 40 men to make Pantins for all his friends. The dolls were brought by the French to colonial America. There they were called Jumping Jacks.

The Pantin on page 11 is wearing a costume from the time of Louis XV, king of France from 1715 to 1774. If you follow the directions on the next pages, you will have two dancing Pantins of your own.

You will need:

scissors   hole punch   ruler   string or yarn   7 paper fasteners

What to do:

1. To make the male Pantin, cut out all the shapes on the next page along outlines.

2. With the hole punch, punch holes wherever there are circles.

3. Cut string or yarn into 5 pieces: two 10-inch pieces, two 7-inch pieces, and one 8-inch piece.

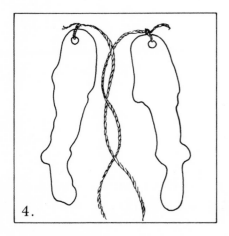

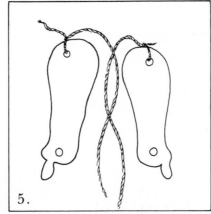

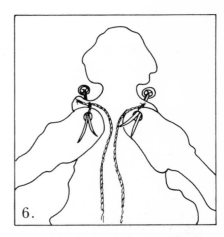

4. Take the Pantin's left arm. Thread one end of a 10-inch string through the hole in it and knot the end of the string above the hole. Tie and knot one end of the other 10-inch string through the hole in the right arm.

5. Take the Pantin's left upper leg. Tie and knot one end of a 7-inch string through hole C. Tie one end of the other 7-inch string through hole D in the right upper leg.

6. Turn the Pantin's body face down. On top of the body lay the left arm, face down,

so hole A in the arm is exactly over hole A in the shoulder. Do the same with the right arm. Put a paper fastener through each hole, so the head of the fastener is on the front of the Pantin. Spread out the backs of the fasteners, making sure they are not too tight.

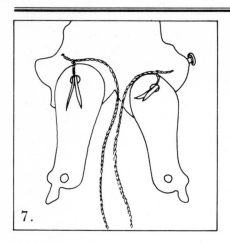

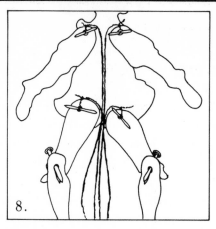

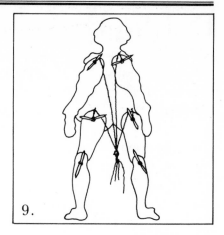

7. Lay the left upper leg over the hip so hole C in the leg is directly over hole C in the hip. Do the same with holes D in the right upper leg and hip. Then fasten both upper legs to the hips with paper fasteners.

8. Letting all the strings hang together as shown, attach the lower legs to the upper legs with fasteners.

9. Pull down all 4 strings together and knot them about an inch below the Pantin's body. The arms and legs should be placed as shown.

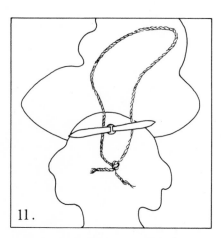

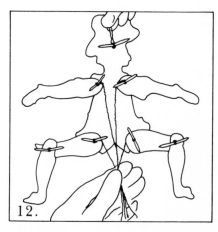

10. Turn the Pantin face up. Put the hat over his head so slit G in the hat is right over slit G in the head. Put a paper fastener through both slits and spread it apart.

11. Turn the Pantin face down again. Take the 8-inch string and loop it around the fastener in the head, then knot it as shown.

12. Hold the head string with one hand, pull the knot with the other, and watch the Pantin dance!

To make the female Pantin on page 13, follow the directions for the male Pantin except:
• You need only 6 paper fasteners.
• Step 3. Cut the string into 4 pieces: two 10-inch and two 7-inch pieces.

• Step 9. Pull down all 4 strings and knot them at the bottom of, not below, the Pantin's skirt. Do not do steps 10 and 11.
• Step 12. Hold the head of the Pantin with one hand, pull the knot with the other, and make the Pantin dance.

RIGHT LOWER LEG

HAT

RIGHT UPPER LEG

LEFT ARM

RIGHT ARM

LEFT UPPER LEG

BODY

LEFT LOWER LEG

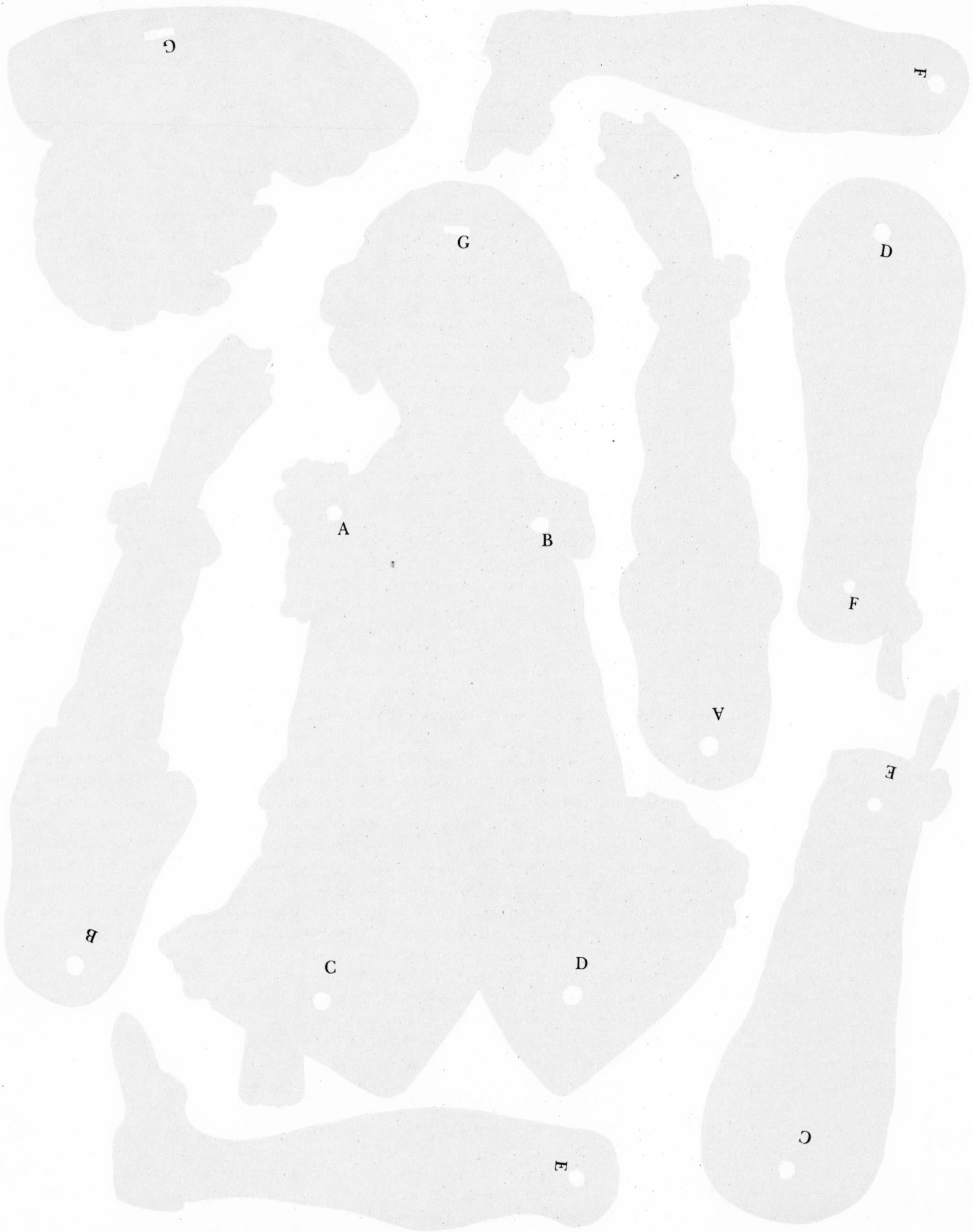
G
F
G
D
A
B
F
A
E
B
C
D
E
C

RIGHT UPPER LEG

LEFT ARM

RIGHT ARM

RIGHT LOWER LEG

LEFT UPPER LEG

BODY

LEFT LOWER LEG

This Pantin in theatrical costume was also printed in France in the 1700s.

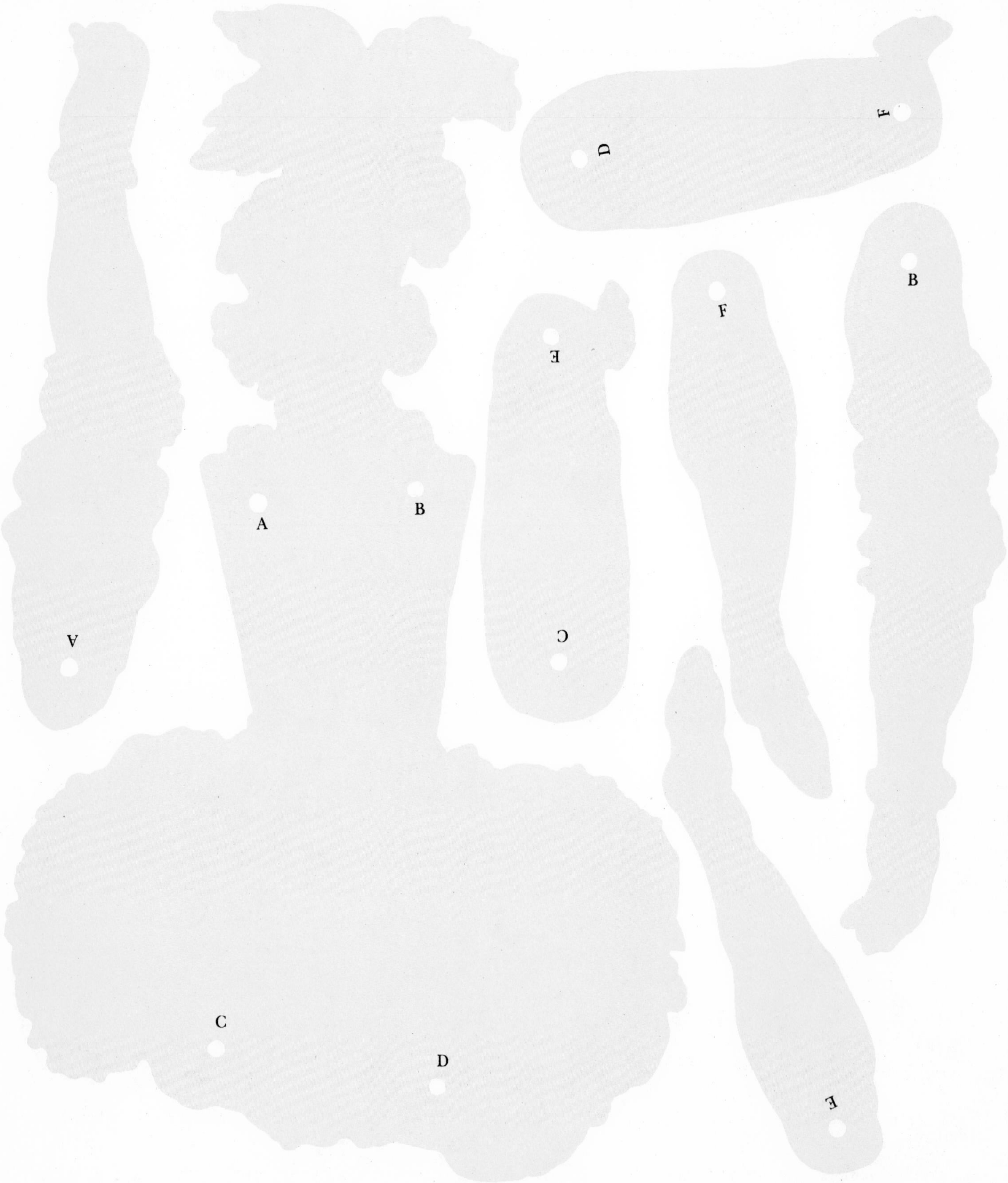

A

B

C

D

E

F

A

B

C

D

E

F

Carp Kite

The carp is a fish that swims against the current, going up streams and waterfalls. To the Japanese the carp symbolizes courage, strength, and success in life. So on May 5 (once called Boys' Day, now called Children's Day) the Japanese fly a carp kite for each son in the family, hoping that their sons will grow up to be brave like the carp.

The carp banner on page 16 (the model for the one you will make) is over 16 feet long. It was made in Kasu, Japan, in 1980 by the shop of Hashimoto Yakichi, which is famous for making carp kites.

A painted kite of the mythical super-boy Kintaro riding a carp, nineteenth-century Japanese.

You will need:

2 sheets of lightweight paper, at least 33 inches long and 18 inches wide. You can use tracing paper, brown craft paper, plain (or the white inside of decorated) wrapping paper, or a very large department store bag.
ruler (a yardstick would be best)
crayons, poster paints, or felt-tip markers
a pole at least 3 feet high (a broom handle, a yardstick, a tree branch)

pencil	pipe cleaner
scissors	string, 12 inches long
white glue	tape

What to do:

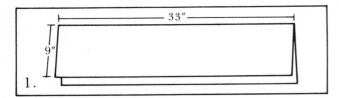

1. Fold paper in half the long way so you have 2 halves, 33 inches long and 9 inches wide.

2. Either draw your own long fish shape, imitating the photograph on page 16, or use a grid to enlarge the outline of that carp onto

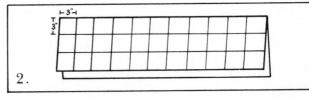

your paper (see p. viii). Using the grid method will help you make a closer copy of the original. If you do use a grid, make squares 3 inches by 3 inches on the folded paper.

3. Decorate carp with bright colors, using either the printed design or your own.

4. Cut out carp along outline, cutting through both sheets of paper.

5. Color in second carp like the first.

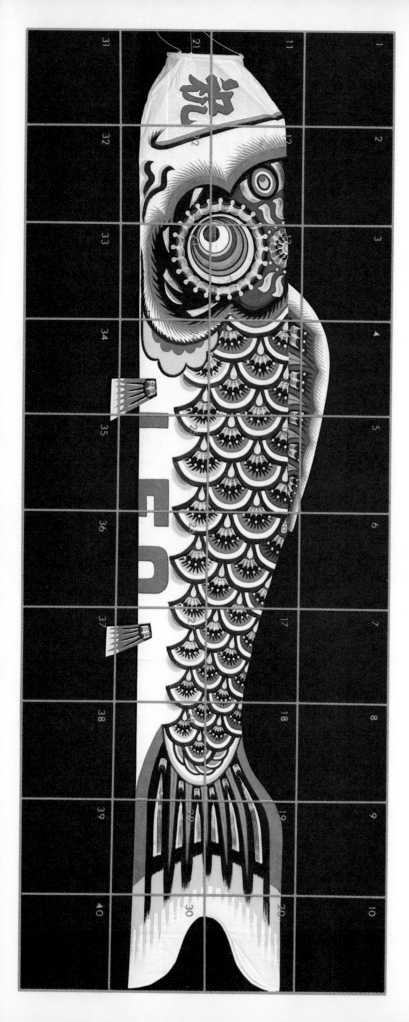

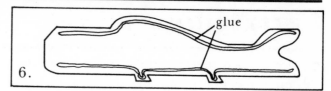

6.

6. Put a long line of glue along the top and bottom edges of the back of one of the carp shapes. Use very little glue or the paper will buckle. Do not spread any glue on the mouth, the tail, or in the middle of the fish.

7.

glue

7. Place other carp shape, colored side up, on top of the first and press down along all the edges. If any glue leaks out, wipe it off.

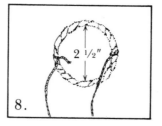

8.

2 ½"

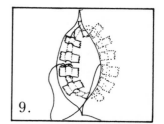

9.

8. Shape pipe cleaner into a circle about 2 ½ inches across. Tie the two ends of the string onto pipe cleaner, directly across from each other.

9. Tape pipe cleaner circle in the mouth of the carp as shown, making sure that the string hangs out the front.

10. Tape or tie the string onto a branch, a stick, a fence, or any pole you can find outside. The carp will fly in the wind, bringing you courage and strength. You can also make the carp fly by running with it, holding it up high behind you.

You can use a large white plastic trash bag to make a carp, but be sure to use permanent felt-tip markers and allow the glue to dry overnight. Homemade carps must come inside when it rains.

Advertising Cards

These cards were popular at the end of the nineteenth century, before the days of radio and television. Stores gave them out to advertise all kinds of products—from shoe leather, corsets, and whisker dye to disposable collars and cuffs, which were then the rage. A suffering person was shown on the card's outside "before" using the product. The card unfolded to show the happy change that came about (cool toes, youthful appearance, marriage proposal accepted) "after" the product was used.

Collecting these cards became a real fad once they began to be printed in color in the 1870s. Children and adults saved the cards and pasted them into scrapbooks. There are many such albums in the museum's collection. The backs of the cards given here are partly blank because they could not be removed from their album.

Solar Tip Shoes and Globe Shirt cards:

1. Cut out the card along outline.

2. Fold up bottom where card is marked "fold."

3. Read the message on the folded card; then open it up to discover how the consumers became happier once they used the product.

Water Lily Soap card:

1. Cut out both sides of card along outline. Glue together back to back so heads face up on both sides.

2. Cut along dotted lines on left and right panels. Stop at the fold lines. Do not cut center panel.

3. Fold each side panel in toward the center along lines marked "fold."

4. You can mix and match the 6 different faces by folding one half of each side at a time into the center. See how many different satisfied Lily Soap users you can create.

You can use these cards as patterns to make your own advertising cards. Draw your own designs and make up your own funny poems. For mix-and-match cards you can cut out faces of people (all of them should be about the same size) from magazines and glue them onto a card like the Water Lily Soap card. Heads or whole bodies of animals can also make very funny cards.

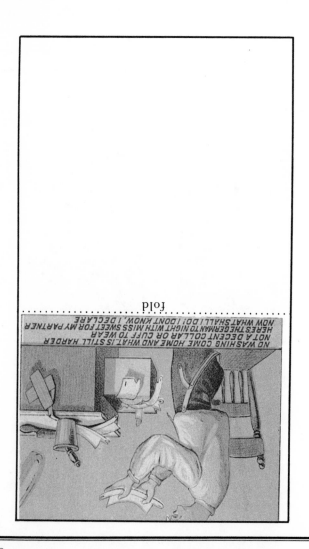

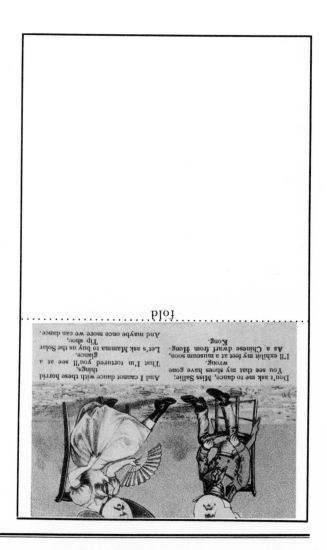

18

SIDE 1

All my clothes are LILY white,
WATER LILY soap made them bright.

I could not use my linen shirt,
But WATER LILY soap would have moved the dirt.

WATER LILY is a fine Toilet Soap
Its pure & white and it will float.

JOSEPH I. KEEP. General Agent
35 SOUTH SECOND STREET,
PHILADELPHIA, PA.

I am very contented as you may tell,
WATER LILY soap moves dirt & smell.

So I'll clap my hands & happy be,
WATER LILY soap is the stuff for me.

SIDE 2

WATER LILY SOAP is free from smell
No rosin mixtures in it dwell.

Alas I'm troubled, blue and sad,
All other Soap but WATER LILY'S bad

Not my portrait you see here,
'Tis the LILY SOAPS maker does appear.

JOSEPH I. KEEP GENERAL AGENT,
35 SOUTH 2ND STREET,
PHILADELPHIA, PA.

To her grocer, she expressed a hope,
That he would keep WATER LILY SOAP.

For the amendment troubles have passed away,
WATER LILY SOAP has come to stay.

Crammed into a Camel

This painting is full of people, rabbits, lions, birds, monkeys—and even a dragon. How sharp are your eyes? See how many people and how many of each of these animals you can find, then check your score against the answer on page 86.

Miniature painting, sixteenth-century Bukharan.

Mystery Objects

Look at the 5 things pictured here. They are small parts of larger objects in the museum. Can you guess what they are? Turn the page to see if you guessed right.

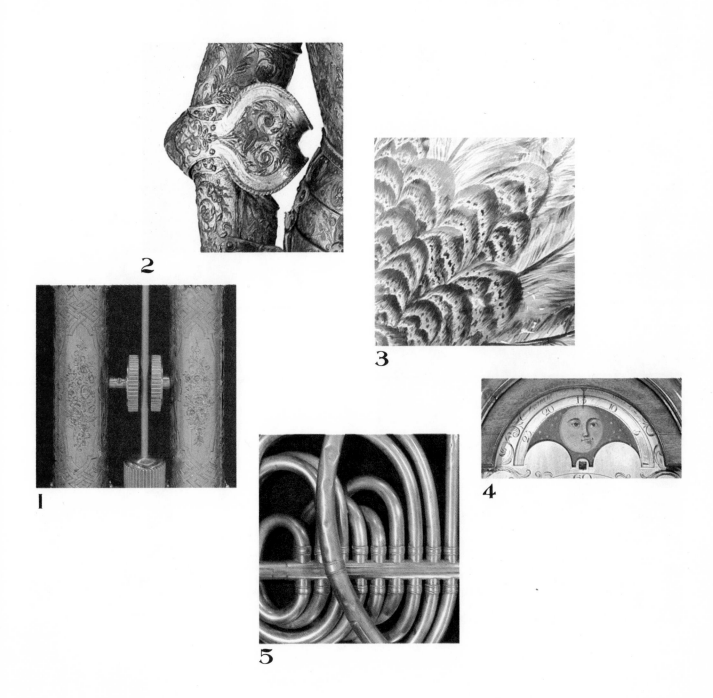

2

1

3

4

5

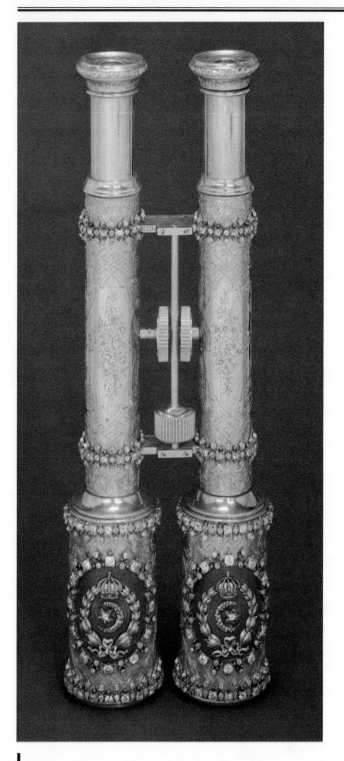

1

These splendid gold field glasses are believed to be from nineteenth-century Switzerland. It is possible that they were made for the Sultan of Turkey, since the crown of Turkey appears at the bottom. They are decorated with diamonds, brass, and enamel.

2

This suit of armor was made in about 1550 for King Henry II of France to wear when he rode in parades. It is made of steel and beautifully embossed and decorated with gold, silver, and brass. It weighs over 53 pounds—a lot more than today's dresswear!

3

This ceramic turkey was made in France in about 1750. He wasn't just decorative—he actually held soup. It was common in the 1700s to serve food in containers shaped like animals.

5

This is an experimental horn made in the early nineteenth century. Its sliding tubes allowed for quick changes in key. This and other experimental horns are the ancestors of our modern French horn.

4

The brass dial shown on page 21 is part of this beautiful mahogany grandfather clock made by Simon Willard in Massachusetts in 1772. Willard was the most famous New England clockmaker of his time. Besides telling the hours of the day, this clock of Willard's also showed how the moon moves across the sky.

Weather Vane

The first known weather vane was made about 25 B.C.E. in Athens, Greece. It was a figure of Triton, a Greek sea god who was half man and half fish. The weather vane stood on top of a 40-foot-high marble tower made to tell time (with a waterclock and sundial) and to measure the winds.

Since then weather vanes have taken many forms. When the first colonists came to America, they brought weather vanes with them from England. In the old country only noblemen could display vanes, but in the free colonies everyone could have one. The rooster was the most popular subject of American weather vanes, but vanes in the shape of ships, animals, Indians, and arrows were also common. They were placed on top of churches and town meeting houses, and shopkeepers also displayed them on their roofs to advertise their trades.

This weather vane in the Metropolitan's collection was on the roof of an American blacksmith's shop in the 1800s. It is made of iron and was painted in bright colors, but the wind and rain wore most of them away.

You will need:

scissors
unlined paper
corrugated cardboard
ruler
a new (unsharpened) pencil
transparent tape

rubber cement
ballpoint pen
a 1-pint cardboard ice cream container or 16-ounce cardboard sour cream or yogurt container, with cover

enough pebbles, marbles, or gravel to fill container
colored paper or cloth
tempera paint, crayons, or felt-tip pens

What to do:

1. Cut out weather vane along outline.

2. Trace around weather vane on unlined paper and cut out shape. This is the back of the weather vane; turn over and decorate.

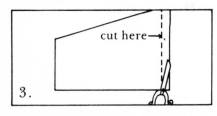

3. Trace around weather vane on corrugated cardboard and cut out shape. Cut off a ½-inch strip from the side of the cardboard as shown.

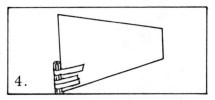

4. Tape one end of the pencil to the cardboard as shown. The pencil should be about halfway up the side of the cardboard.

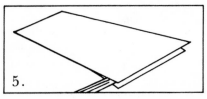

5. Glue or dry mount (see p. vii) front of weather vane onto cardboard. Glue or dry mount back of weather vane onto other side of cardboard. The pencil should be hidden between the two sides.

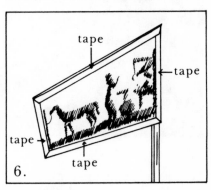

6. Tape front and back of weather vane together around all edges.

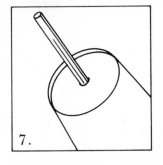

7.

9.

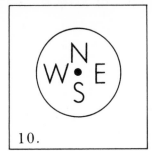

10.

11.

7. With the ballpoint pen, punch a hole in the center of the bottom of container. Remove pen.

8. The container is the base of the weather vane—glue on colored paper or cloth and decorate it.

9. Fill container with pebbles, marbles, or gravel. Tape cover on in at least 4 places and turn upside down.

10. Around the hole mark north, south, east, and west with a ballpoint pen as shown.

11. Push pencil into hole and jiggle it around until it spins freely.

12. Set your weather vane down on level ground. When the horse faces north, the wind is coming from the south; when he faces east, it is blowing from the west; and so on. Use your weather vane to show where the wind is coming from.

Stained Glass

Stained glass window making has been called the art of painting with light. Stained glass was most popular in the twelfth and thirteenth centuries in Europe. Large stained glass windows were made for cathedrals by glaziers (GLAY-zhurs). The glaziers first drew a cartoon, or picture, of the finished window. Then they made glass and colored it, sometimes painting on fine details where needed. Next they made a large pattern for the window and cut the glass to fit the pattern. The glaziers outlined the glass pieces with lead, joined the lead pieces together, attached iron bars for strength, and set the window into the wall of the building.

In modern times (the last 100 years) artists like Louis Comfort Tiffany and John La Farge designed stained glass windows for private homes and public buildings. Now you can make your own "stained glass."

A sixteenth-century German window commemorating a marriage.

You will need:

scissors   tracing paper
white glue   felt-tip pens

What to do:

1. Tear out pages 28 and 29 along perforations.

2. Cut out only the areas marked. If the tail and base are too hard to cut out, leave them as they are.

3. Glue the front and back of the griffin together, where marked.

4. Place tracing paper over griffin and separately trace each of the 4 sections along the outer and inner edges of the outline.

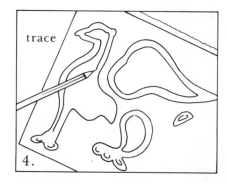

5. Color each section differently. Each section does not have to be a solid color; you can draw designs within it to make it look like La Farge's

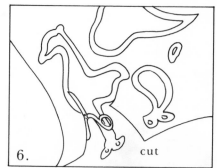

stained glass, or you can draw your own designs.

6. Cut out each section along outside edge.

(Continued on page 28)

cut here

Glue tracing paper along these lines.

Glue tracing paper along these lines.

cut here

here

cut here

here

Glue tracing paper along these lines.

cut here

here

cut here

Glue tracing paper along these lines.

here

cut here

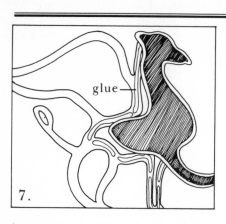

7.

7. Turn griffin over. Carefully put glue on griffin along outline of one section and paste down the tracing paper with the back of your design facing you. Let dry.

8. Paste down one section at a time, allowing it to dry before putting down the next one.

9. When all the sections are pasted down and dry, turn the griffin face up, hold it up to the light, and admire your stained glass window!

Ask your parents for permission to tape the griffin onto a window so sunlight will shine through. Watch the griffin change color from hour to hour as the color of the daylight changes.

Try making your own stained glass windows by cutting shapes out of black paper and gluing in colored "glass." Remember, the simplest shapes are often the nicest. Instead of tracing paper for "glass," you can use thick clear plastic food wrap for microwave cooking or self-sealing food storage bags, which can be colored with permanent felt-tip markers (watercolor markers won't work). Colored tissue paper also makes lovely stained glass.

cut here

ut here

cut here

"Lunette" by John La Farge, 1882. The griffins in this window were models for the one given here. La Farge, an American, created over 1,000 stained glass windows.

Unicorn Tapestry Word Find

In about 1500 a series of 7 tapestries showing the hunt of a unicorn was woven. These were some of the finest wall hangings made in the Middle Ages. In the tapestry shown here the unicorn is purifying a pool of water so the animals nearby can drink safely. The person who designed the tapestries included many different animals, people, and more than 100 kinds of plants, all blooming at once. Can you find the CASTLE, FOUNTAIN, HOUND, LION, ORANGES, RABBIT, and UNICORN in the tapestry? Then look for those words in the puzzle at right. To spell out each word, draw a line from one letter to another. You can go up, down, left, right, and on a slant—just don't jump over any letter. One word has been done for you. The answer is on page 86.

```
G  P  A  K  F  H  C  M
U  N  I  C  O  R  N  C
T  O  B  D  U  N  A  S
I  I  L  Q  N  S  O  T
B  F  F  V  T  U  J  A
B  R  D  L  A  U  O  G
A  I  E  S  I  T  E  L
Q  S  E  G  N  A  R  O
```

"The Unicorn at the Fountain," anonymous.

Wall Hanging

Look closely at the shirt or blouse you are wearing. Can you see tiny threads in a crisscross pattern? Those threads were most probably woven with thousands of other threads on a huge power-driven loom that made enough cloth at one time for hundreds of shirts like yours.

Down through the ages, though, people spun and wove their own fabrics by hand. Prehistoric people wove baskets from grasses. When they began to move from place to place looking for food, they built shelters by weaving together tree branches, grasses, and reeds. Egyptians used looms to weave their clothes from cotton, linen, and wool more than 5,000 years ago. They wrapped their mummies only with woven linen, which was their finest material.

In medieval times tapestries, or very large wall hangings, were woven to decorate castle walls and to keep the castles warm. On the facing page is one of the unicorn tapestries, very beautiful wall hangings from that period. Turn to page 35 to see a special Chinese silk tapestry that was woven by very skilled craftsmen.

Today, even though much cloth is made in factories, people in many countries still weave by hand. In the United States, Native Americans make beautiful rugs and clothing on looms. And other artists weave objects of every shape and size and make them into wall hangings, sculptures, and things that we can use.

This model of a weaving shop was made in Egypt almost 4,000 years ago. You can see that the Egyptians wove on looms very much like the ones used today!

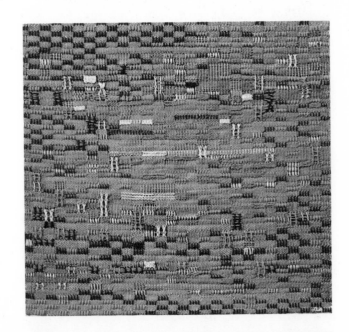

Green ribbon weaving by Anni Albers called "Pasture," 1958 (detail).

The loom:

Before you start weaving, you will need to know about the different parts of your loom:

The WARP THREADS are attached to the loom from top to bottom before you start to weave.

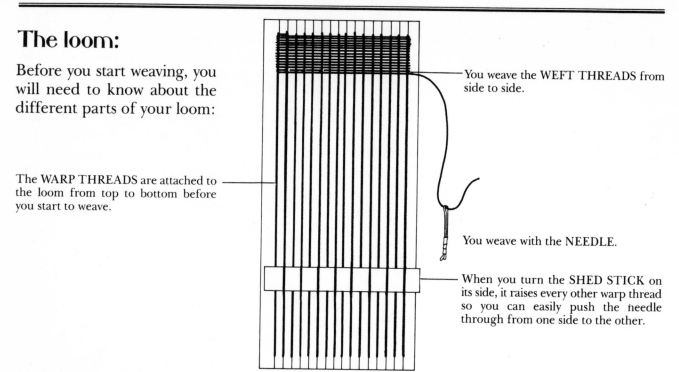

You weave the WEFT THREADS from side to side.

You weave with the NEEDLE.

When you turn the SHED STICK on its side, it raises every other warp thread so you can easily push the needle through from one side to the other.

You will need:

a Styrofoam tray—you can get these in the supermarket when you buy meat, fish, or vegetables. If you ask the person who works behind the meat counter for one or two clean trays, he or she will probably give them to you. On the bottom of the trays are code numbers that stand for the size of the tray. The best sizes for weaving are 10S, 10D, 12S, 12D, 16S, and 16D trays.

scissors
ruler
pencil
3- or 4-ply yarn, different colors, 45 feet in all
2 ½-inch bobby pin
masking tape
a new (unsharpened) pencil
white glue

What to do:

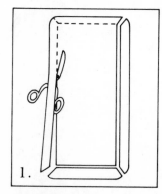

1.

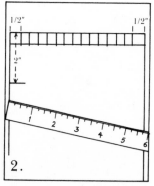

2.

1. Cut off all 4 sides of the tray along bottom edge. *Keep the side pieces.* The bottom of the tray will be your loom.

2. Begin with the bottom of the tray. Place the ruler ½ inch down from the top edge and draw a line across from left to right. Measure ½ inch from the left side. Mark that point. Then, starting from that point, measure and mark ¼-inch points all along the top line, stopping ½ inch from the right side. Make sure you have an even number of marks. Do the same along the bottom edge. Mark a point on the left side 2 inches down from the top, and another on the right side, 2 inches up from the bottom.

3. With scissors, cut into the Styrofoam at all the points you have marked, as shown.

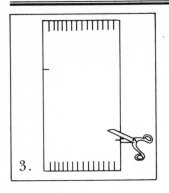

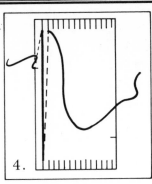

3. 4.

7. Cut 6 feet of the color yarn you want to begin weaving with. Put the end of the yarn through the eye of the bobby pin. Wrap tape around the open end of the pin. This is your needle. You are now ready to begin weaving.

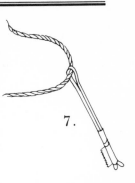

7.

4. Cut a piece of yarn about 24 feet long. While you are threading your loom, make sure the curve of the tray (if any) faces you. Put one end of the yarn through the notch 2 inches down on the left side, front to back, leaving a loose end of about 3 inches. Bring the yarn around the back through the first top notch, then down to the first notch on the bottom. Wrap it around the back of the loom and through the second notch on top.

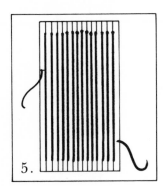

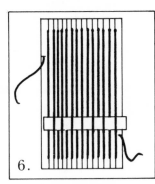

5. 6.

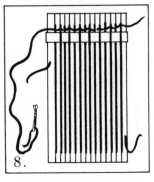

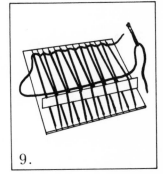

8. 9.

5. Bring the yarn down to the second notch on bottom, behind the loom to the top third notch, and so on until you finish lacing the last notch on the bottom right corner. Put the end of the yarn through the notch 2 inches up on the right side, leave about 3 inches, and cut the yarn. You have just placed the warp threads on your loom.

6. Cut a piece as wide as the loom from the edge of the tray that you cut off in step 1. This is the shed stick. Insert it into the warp threads from the right side by weaving it under the first warp thread, over the second, under the third, and so on as shown.

8. Starting from the top right side, weave the needle over the first warp thread, under the second thread, over the third, under the fourth, and so on until the end of the warp. Pull the yarn through, leaving about 3 extra inches on the right side. This completes the first row of weft threads. With the shed stick, push the weft up to the very top of the loom.

9. To weave the second line, turn shed stick on its side.

10. Push needle through from left to right.

11. Turn shed stick back down flat and use it to push the second line of weft to the top of loom. Make sure yarn is packed tightly. Move shed stick back down to center of loom.

12. Weaving every line of weft from right to left will be the same: weave the yarn over the first warp thread, under the second, and so on. Push the weft up with the shed stick. Weaving every line from left to right will be the same: turn the shed stick on its side, push the needle through, turn the shed stick flat, use it to push the weft up to the top of the loom, and move it back to center. This is how you will weave the whole piece.

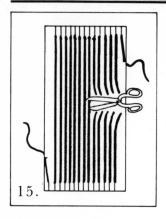
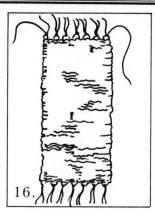
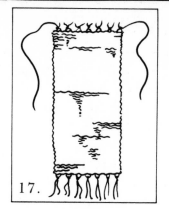
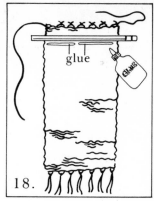

15.

16.

17.

18.

glue

13. When you are about to run out of yarn, cut a new piece 6 feet long and tie the end of it to the yarn in the loom. Make the knot tight and cut off the ends.

14. When you are weaving the last few lines, you will have to remove the shed stick. Continue to weave until you reach the bottom of the loom. Cut the yarn when you finish the last line, leaving an end of 3 inches. Knot end of yarn around last warp thread and trim end.

15. Turn loom over. Cut all the warp threads in half.

16. Pull the warp threads out from between the notches at top and bottom. On the top edge tie the first and second threads to-

gether. Tie the third and fourth together, and so on until all are tied. Do the same on the bottom edge.

17. Cut the top fringe off above the knots *except for the piece at the extreme left and the one at the extreme right.*

18. Turn the hanging over. Lay the pencil across the weaving about 1 inch from the top and put a lot of glue on the weaving under the pencil. Wrap the top of the hanging around the pencil and press the wool onto the glue. Let dry.

19. Put tape along the edge as shown. Tie the two ends of the fringe together and your weaving is ready for hanging!

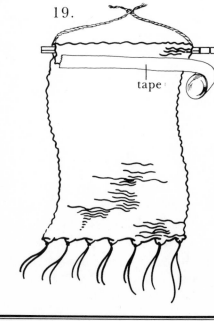

19.

tape

You can weave hangings out of ribbons, straws, raffia, strips of paper, rolled-up aluminum foil, string, shoelaces, and fabric. If you want to make something useful, you can make a bookmark, coaster, pot holder, or dollhouse rug. With the largest size Styrofoam tray (supermarkets call it the economy size), you can weave placemats.

Birds Galore

This tapestry was made in China between 1600 and 1650. It is 7 feet high and is woven with silk and gold threads. The designs in the blue band across the top are good luck symbols. The bird in the center is the mythical *fêng huang,* the king of birds and the symbol of happiness. An ancient legend tells us that when the *fêng huang* flies, 100 birds follow it, and when the *fêng huang* dies, all the birds bury it. The artist could not include all 100 birds in the tapestry but he did have 18 (including the *fêng huang*) woven into the design. The birds include a crane, pheasants, a peacock, a goose, an egret, mandarin ducks, a paradise flycatcher, swallows, and magpies. Can you find the 18 birds?

The answer is on page 86.

Optical Toys

When we watch movies, we are really looking at a series of individual pictures, one quickly following another. We do not notice the brief space between the pictures—our eyes continue to see one image until the next appears. Our brains are fooled into thinking that instead of separate pictures, there is just one that is moving. This is called persistence of vision and was discovered early in the nineteenth century.

In that century a number of optical toys were invented that made use of persistence of vision. One such toy was the Mutoscope. People looked through a small window on the front of the Mutoscope. When they turned a side handle, a movie appeared in the window. The movie was really a stack of cards attached to a wheel. On the cards were photographs of people in different stages of movement. Cranking the handle turned the wheel, which flipped the cards over quickly, making the photographs look like a moving picture. Children and adults made pocket-sized Mutoscopes for their home entertainment. These were called flicker or flip books. You can make your own flip book by following the directions below.

Flip Book

When you flip the pages of this little book, men appear to be playing leapfrog and a horse seems to be running. The photographs of both were taken by Eadweard Muybridge, one of the first photographers to re-create motion with a camera. And he did it partly because of a bet. In 1872 Governor Leland Stanford of California hired Muybridge to win a bet. Governor Stanford had bet that when a horse gallops, all four of its feet leave the ground at some point. Stanford wanted Muybridge to prove this was so by photographing the horse as it ran.

You will need: scissors   stapler

What to do:

1. Cut out each picture of leapfrog along outlines. You will have 18 numbered rectangles.
2. Put pictures in a stack in numerical order, face up, with #1 on top and #18 on bottom.
3. Staple cards together where marked. The

Muybridge set up a row of 24 cameras along a racetrack, attached a string to each camera, and then laid the strings across the track. As a horse galloped down the track it broke each string, which made each camera take a picture. Muybridge got 24 pictures of the galloping horse. Sure enough, all the horse's feet came off the ground at one point. Stanford won his bet, and Muybridge went on to photograph people and animals of every kind in motion.

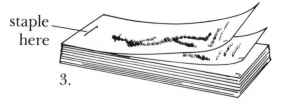

staple here

3.

more exactly the photographs are lined up, the better the flip book will work.

4. Flip cards from front to back and watch grown men playing leapfrog.
5. Turn the flipbook over, flip it from front to back, and watch the horse and rider amble down the road.

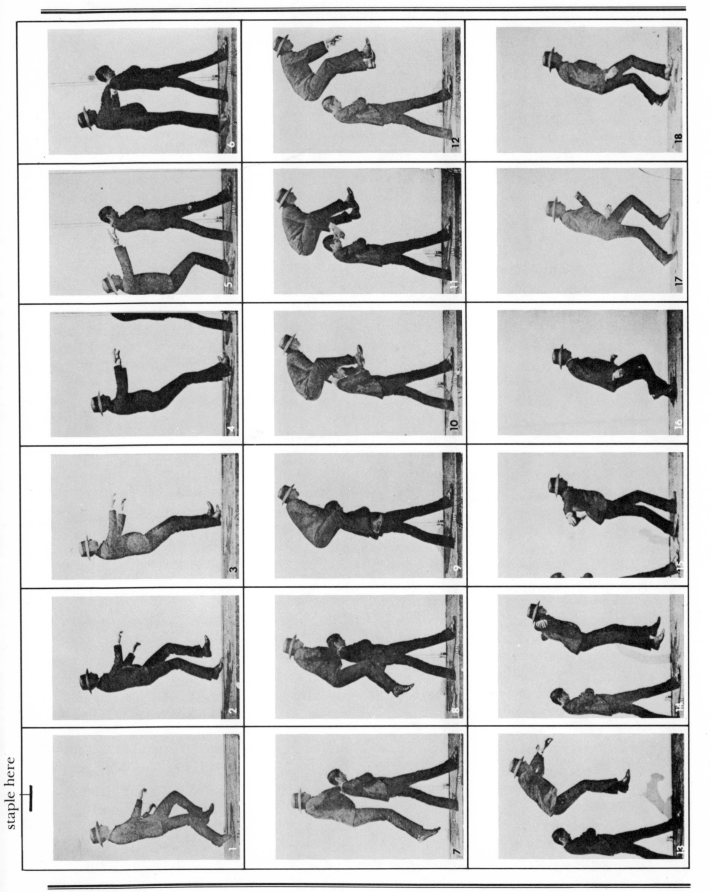

Leapfrog

The Amble

Zoetrope

The zoetrope (ZOE-ee-trope) was a popular moving-picture toy invented around 1837. Zoetrope strips like those on page 41 were used with the toy to make short movies.

Muybridge also used the zoetrope. He put his pictures of horses into the toy and spun it to make the horses "run."

You will need:

scissors	compass	paper clip	paper or plastic cup with a
transparent tape	light cardboard	small bead	flat bottom

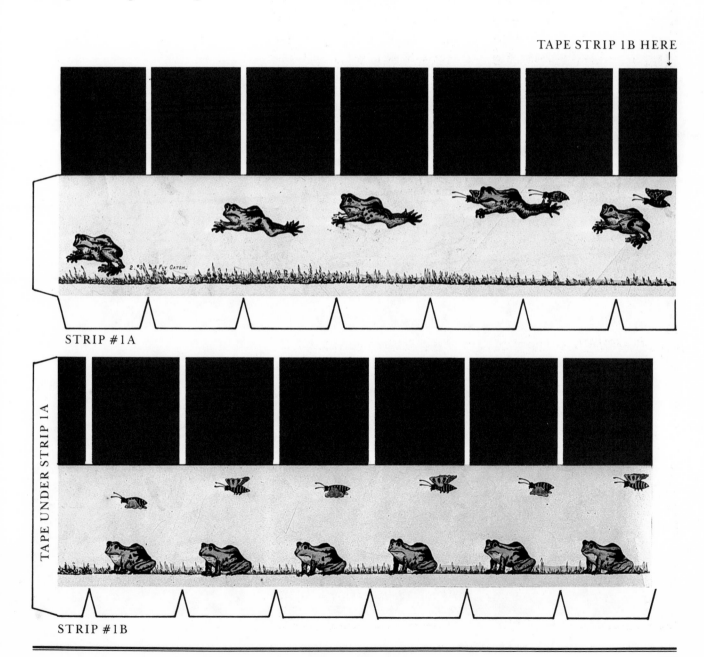

TAPE STRIP 1B HERE

STRIP #1A

TAPE UNDER STRIP 1A

STRIP #1B

What to do:

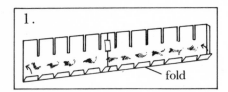

1.

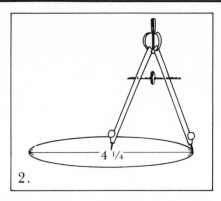

2.

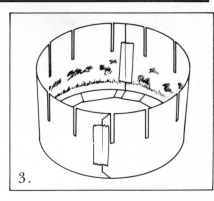

3.

1. Cut out both parts of strip #1, tape the ends together, and fold up bottom tabs as shown.

2. Using the compass, draw a circle 4 ¼ inches across on the cardboard. Cut out the circle. This will be the base.

3. Tape the ends of strip #1 together as shown so that frogs are inside and solid color is outside.

STRIP #2A   TAPE STRIP 2B HERE ↑

TAPE UNDER STRIP 2A   STRIP #2B

STRIP #3A   TAPE STRIP 3B HERE ↑

TAPE UNDER STRIP 3A   STRIP #3B

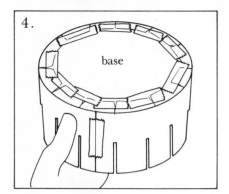

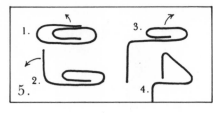

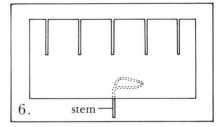

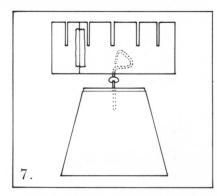

4. Drop round base into the cylinder formed by the taped strip. Tape the two together underneath as shown.

5. Unfold paper clip as shown.

6. Push the stem of the clip through the center of base.

7. Slide bead onto the part of the stem that sticks out below the base. Then push the beaded stem through the center of the overturned cup.

STRIP #4A

STRIP #4B

STRIP #5A

STRIP #5B

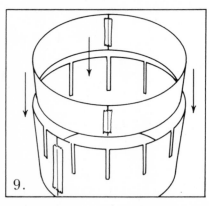

9.

8. Holding the dark squares at eye level, look through the slits at the opposite wall, then spin the cylinder. Watch the figures inside move!

9. To make more moving pictures, cut out both parts of strip #2, tape them together, and then tape the ends of the long strip together so the paper forms a ring with the acrobats on the inside. Drop the ring into your already made zoetrope as shown and spin again.

10. Slip out strip #2, cut the tape, and turn the ring inside out—so the jumping horses (strip #4) are inside the ring this time. Retape the ends, drop the ring into the zoetrope, and spin. You can do the same with strips #3 and 5. First the monkeys and dogs will show inside the zoetrope, then the cats and mice.

Now that you know how to make a zoetrope, why not make your own pictures? Draw them on a horizontal strip the same size as the ones given here. Pick something that moves a little bit in each picture. Then watch your drawings come to life!

Perplexing Paths

H ere are four mazes from the 1728 book *New Principles of Gardening* by Batty Langley, an English garden designer. These contain "strait, angular, circular, and rural walks." Start at the pond in the center. Can you find your way through the upper right maze, then the upper left maze and the lower left maze to the pool in the middle of the lower right one? The answer is on page 86.

Japanese Paper Dolls

In the late 1800s the Japanese became very interested in the culture of Westerners, including Western clothing. They read European fashion magazines and dressed in European-style clothes. Japanese artists made fashion prints, which may have been copied from illustrations in Western magazines. Some of the prints became paper dolls, like those shown on the following pages. These prints were made in 1898. The man is shown here with his traditional robe, or kimono (kee-MOE-noe), as well as a Western suit and hats. The woman has traditional kimonos and wigs.

You will need: scissors   rubber cement   light cardboard   transparent tape

What to do:

1. Cut out backs and fronts of woman and man along outlines.

2. Glue or dry mount (see p. vii) back of woman to front of woman and back of man to front of man.

3. Cut out man's arm, then glue to man as shown.

4. Cut out stand, trace onto

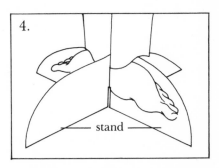

cardboard, and cut out shape. Notch slot in cardboard stand

into slot on bottom of figure. Repeat with other figure.

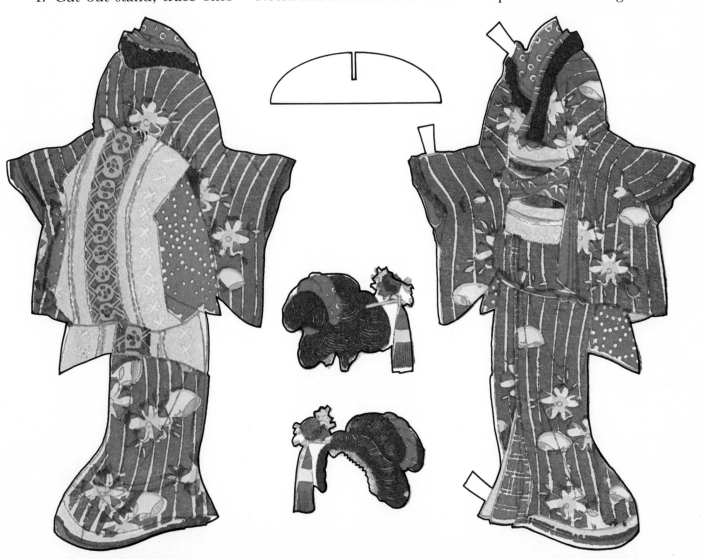

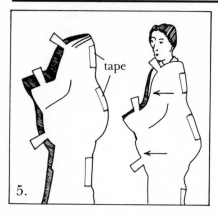

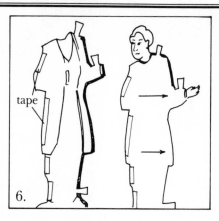

5. Cut out clothes, front and back. Tape the front of the woman's clothes to the back along right edge as shown. Then slide clothes on from the right and turn tabs down at left.

6. Do the same with the man's clothes, taping along left edge and folding down tabs at right.

7. For hats and wigs, glue fronts and backs together along all edges except bottom, then slide onto head as shown.

fold and glue together

The Temple of Dendur

The temple of Dendur was built around 21–20 B.C.E., in a country just south of Egypt called Nubia (NOO-bee-a), on the banks of the Nile River. The Nubians built the temple as a monument to two young princes, Pihor and Pedisi, who had drowned in the Nile. It was also a temple dedicated to the goddess Isis. The walls were decorated with figures of Isis, her son Horus, many other gods, the two brothers, the pharaoh, animals, and plants. The Nubians carved hieroglyphs (ancient Egyptian writing) next to the figures to describe them. You can see the hieroglyph for Horus, the winged disk, on the entrance to each of the three chambers of the temple. Horus protected the doorways of Egyptian temples.

The innermost chamber of the temple was very sacred, and only priests were allowed to enter it. The carving on the back wall shows Pihor, Pedisi, the goddess Isis, and her husband, the god Osiris. The back wall of the temple is very thick, and hidden inside is a small, empty secret chamber. One of the stones on the outer wall opened up to allow someone to crawl into the chamber. Scholars think that the coffins of one or two of the brothers may have been kept there, but no one knows for sure. It is one of the mysteries of the temple of Dendur. Turn to page 51 to see how you can build a model of this famous temple.

You will need: scissors   glue

The temple at its original site on the Nile River, Nubia.   It was given to the United States by the Egyptian government and now stands in a special wing at the Metropolitan Museum.

Harvester Word Find

The harvesters are pausing to have their noonday meal. Nearby are a BASKET, BIRDS, a CHURCH, a LADDER, a SCYTHE (a curved blade), WHEAT, and a WINE JUG. First try to find these things in the painting. Then hunt for these words in the puzzle at right. To spell out each word, draw a line from one letter to another. You can go up, down, left, right, and on a slant—but you can't jump over any letter. One word has been done for you. The answer is on page 87.

```
T E H T Y C S A
E S G L W H G Q
K G R F K U S J
S B A T J R D B
A C N E O C R P
C U N V H H I E
H I A M E W B D
W Z R E D D A L
```

"The Harvesters" by Pieter Bruegel the Elder, Flemish, 1565.

Versailles Redesigned

This is Langley's plan for redoing the labyrinth at Versailles (vair-SIGH), France, a palace that was built for King Louis XIV in the mid-seventeenth century. Langley's sketch added many twists and turns to the maze. Even without these imaginary complications, it was the most elaborate maze of the time. Pumping water from the Seine River to the many sculpted fountains in the maze was enormously expensive.

Start in the lower left corner and see if you can find your way past the statues, fountains, and orchards to the lower right corner. The answer is on page 87.

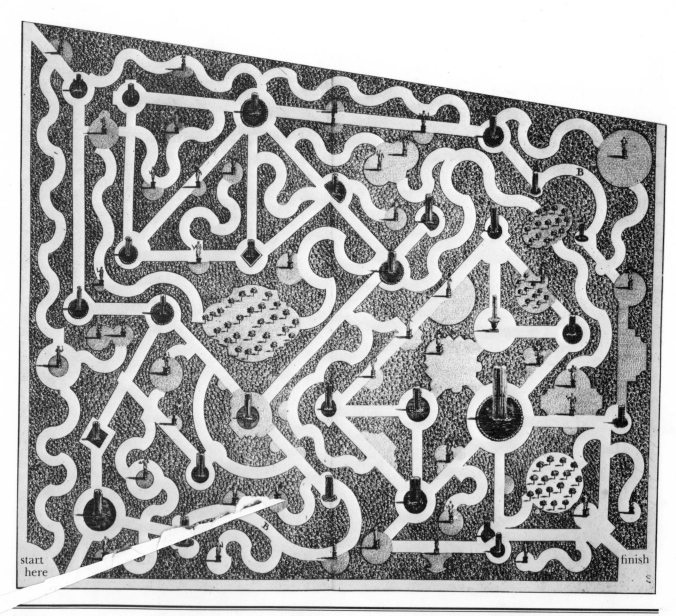

start here

finish

Mosaic

This hare may look young, but he is really 2,000 years old! He is a mosaic made of glass tiles that was made in Rome in the first century B.C.E. As early as 500 B.C.E. mosaics made of small stones were used to decorate the floors of houses in Greece. Later they decorated walls in houses, public buildings, and churches throughout Europe.

Mosaics are made up of small pieces that do not seem to be important when they are seen alone. But when they are put together with many other small pieces in a creative way, they can be great works of art.

You will need:

corrugated cardboard   rubber cement
scissors   white glue
transparent tape
dried beans—these may be yellow and green
    split peas, chick peas, lentils, red or white
    kidney beans, lima, pinto, coffee, navy, black
    turtle soup beans, or any others you can find.
pasta—such as white linguini, spinach spaghetti, wheat spaghetti, elbow macaroni,
    bowties, vermicelli, rice of all kinds
seeds—such as sunflower seeds, watermelon
    seeds, pistachio nutshells, bird seed,
    pumpkin seeds
containers for seeds—such as muffin tins,
    paper or plastic cups, jar lids
clear acrylic spray (optional)

What to do:

1. Tear out page 63. Cut a piece of corrugated cardboard 8 ¾ by 10 ¾ inches.

2. Glue or dry mount (see p. vii) page onto cardboard. Let dry.

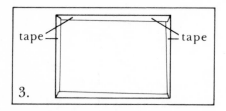

3. Tape each edge of the page to the cardboard to prevent curling (see p. vii).

4. Pour each different kind of bean, pasta, or seed into a separate container. Be sure that you keep the colors separate from one another.

5. Decide which color, type, and size piece you want to use for each area. Round shapes might work better for a curved space, tiny round or straight shapes for a long, skinny area.

6. Squeeze out enough glue on the paper for only a small area at a time. Begin by gluing and putting down the pieces along the outline of an area. Fill in the shape with pieces of the same, or almost the same, color. Use different colors for the eyes and nose of the rabbit and for the lizard's eye. Try making the tops of the mushrooms a different color from the stems. (And small pieces of spaghetti make lovely rabbit whiskers!)

Using one color, or different shades of one color, for each shape will make the shapes stand out. For instance, if you make the rabbit white, beige, and light yellow, and the plants different shades of green, the rabbit and plants will stand out from one another. But if you make the rabbit white, green, and yellow, and the plants green, white, and yellow, you won't be able to tell which is which. Fill in all sections of picture.

7. Finish covering each section of wet glue before you move on to another section. Do not put down glue in a large area (it will dry too fast) and do not put down big blobs of glue (they will make the paper wrinkle).

8. When you have finished your mosaic, let the glue dry overnight. Spray it with clear acrylic fixer, or mix a bit of white glue with 3 times as much water, stir well, and lightly brush the mixture over your mosaic. Let dry. This will make the mosaic last longer and will keep insects and animals away.

Draw your own pictures directly onto corrugated cardboard to make into mosaics. Keep them simple, drawing mostly outlines of shapes. You can also use bits of colored paper to make mosaics. Or punch holes in construction paper with a hole punch and use all the dots. Or cut gift wrap, newspaper, and magazine pages into squares, triangles, and circles and use them in a mosaic. Washers, nuts, and bolts also make good mosaic materials. So do buttons and beads. Mosaics can be made with just about anything, but mostly with a good imagination!

Three Heads Are Better Than One

Agnolo di Cosimo di Mariano, also called Bronzino, was an artist who lived in Florence, Italy, from 1503 to 1572. He painted many portraits of aristocratic men and women and made most of them seem to stare icily out into the world. No one knows for sure who the young man in this painting is. Look carefully at the painting and see if you can find 2 other faces. The answer is on page 87.

What to do:

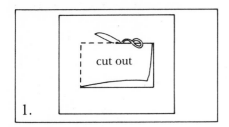 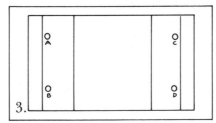 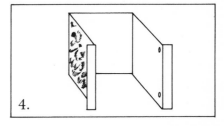

1. Cut out the theater frame as shown.

2. Cut out the theater back on page 75.

3. Take the hole punch and make holes in circles A, B, C, and D.

4. Decorate blank theater back. Then fold it as shown. Make sure to press firmly along each crease.

THEATER FRAME

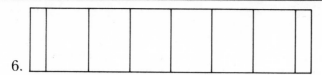

6.

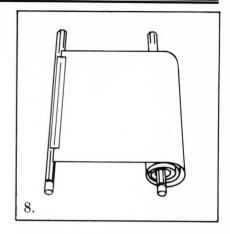

8.

5. Cut a strip of paper 4 by 18 1/2 in. If you don't have paper that long, cut two strips that are each 4 by 9 1/4 in. and glue them together with the rubber cement.

6. With the pencil and ruler, rule a 1-inch margin at the top and the bottom of the paper strip. Then divide the rest of the strip into 6 boxes, each 2 3/4 inches high. These boxes will be the scenes of your play.

7. Make up your own play. Draw a scene in each of the 6 boxes. If your play needs more than 6 scenes, just glue more 4-inch-wide paper to the end of your strip and rule it into boxes that are 2 3/4 inches high. Remember to leave a 1-inch margin at the end of the new strip.

8. Tape each end of the strip to the center of a pencil. Roll most of the paper onto one pencil as shown.

GLUE HERE

GLUE HERE

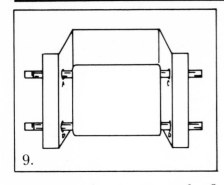

9.

9. Insert the eraser end of one pencil into hole A on the theater back. Insert the other end of that pencil into hole C. Insert the second pencil into holes B and D as shown.

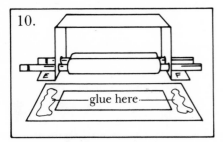

10.

glue here

10. Glue sides E and F of the theater back to the back of the theater frame as shown.

11. Now your theater is finished. By turning the top pencil away from you, you can make each scene appear on stage. Turn the bottom pencil toward you to rewind the play and begin again.

You might want to write and perform several plays in different kinds of theaters. Shoe boxes, gift boxes, and cardboard cartons make wonderful theaters. When making a larger theater, instead of pencils use the cardboard tubes from rolls of plastic wrap or aluminum foil.

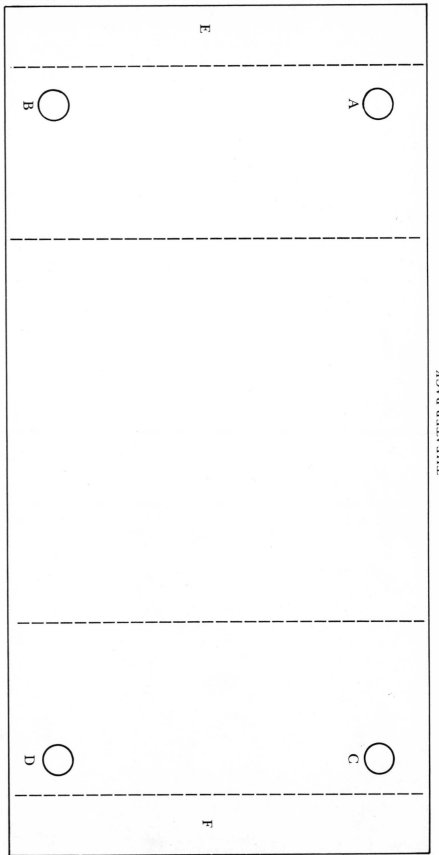

E

B

A

THEATER BACK

D

C

F

Marine Life Word Find

Hundreds of plants and animals live under the sea. In this watercolor of underwater life you can see the great variety of their shapes and colors. First look in the painting for the CRAB, EEL, FISH, LOBSTERS, SEAHORSE, SEAWEED, SHELL, SNAIL, and STARFISH. Then hunt for those words in the puzzle at right. To spell out each word, draw a line from one letter to another. You can go up, down, left, right, and on a slant—but you can't jump over any letter. One word has been done for you. The answer is on page 87.

```
K  S  I  F  X  N  S  L
H  E  E  L  H  C  L  I
O  A  G  M  R  E  R  A
I  H  R  A  H  L  B  N
L  O  B  S  T  E  R  S
A  W  E  S  H  A  U  E
E  E  I  F  R  Q  T  S
S  E  D  B  L  R  I  F
```

"Underwater Marine Life" by Christian Schuessele and James Somerville, American, late nineteenth century.

Panpipe (A difficult project for older or more experienced readers)

Panpipes have been played for centuries all over the world in ceremonies, festivals, and for fun. They are made of bamboo, stone, clay, wood, and even metal. The first panpipes came from ancient China. They were taken by traveling musicians from China to Korea to Japan.

The illustration is a 100-year-old copy of an ancient Japanese panpipe. It has 12 pipes, one for each of the 12 notes in Chinese and Japanese music. There is a Chinese and Japanese scale (called the pentatonic scale) that uses only 5 of the 12 notes. The panpipe you will make has 5 pipes, one for each note of the pentatonic scale.

You will need:

plastic shower rod covering, found in hardware, bathroom furnishing, and novelty stores. It comes in 5-foot lengths.
5 corks from wine bottles—you can also find corks in crafts stores.
yardstick
pencil

scissors
transparent tape
masking tape
felt-tip pens, crayons, or tempera paints
light cardboard
rubber cement or white glue

What to do:

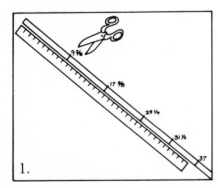

1. Lay the shower rod next to the yardstick. With the pencil, mark the tube next to the 9 3/8 mark on the ruler. Do the same at 17 5/8 inches, 25 1/4 inches, 31 1/2 inches,

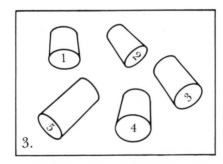

and 37 inches (one inch beyond the end of the yardstick).

2. Cut the tube where you've marked. You'll end up with 5 tubes. Their lengths will be 9 3/8 inches, 8 1/4 inches,

7 5/8 inches, 6 1/4 inches, and 5 1/2 inches.

3. Number the bottoms of the corks 1, 2, 3, 4, 5.

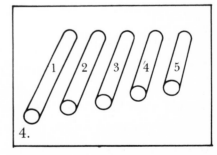

4. Line up tubes as shown. The longest will be #1, the next #2, and so on.

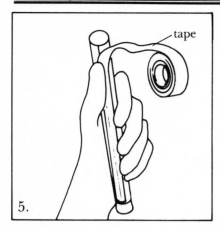

5. Put cork #1 in the end of tube #1 so about half the cork sticks out the bottom. Press the tube together with one hand so the tube winds tightly around the cork. With your other hand, tape the tube closed with the transparent tape as shown.

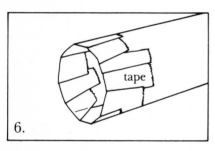

6. Put a layer of transparent tape around the open end of tube #1 as shown. Then put another layer over the first.

7. Put cork #2 into tube #2, tape the tube closed, and tape the opening. Do the same for tubes #3, #4, and #5.

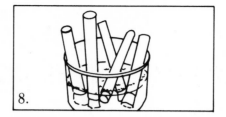

8. If the corks are very loose in the tubes, stand the corked tubes in enough water to cover the corks as shown. Soak them overnight. The corks will expand to fit tightly in the tubes.

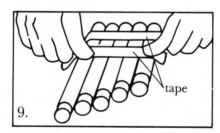

9. Making sure the open tops are in a straight line, tape the tubes together twice with masking tape. Wrap the ends of the tape around the back of the tubes.

10. Turn tubes over and tape the other side in the same way.

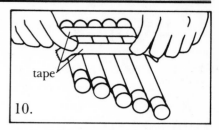

11. Cut out the case-front along outline. Trace the shape onto light cardboard and cut out shape. This is the case-back for you to decorate. You can copy the case-front or make your own design. Then color it and paste on fabric, buttons, foil, or anything that appeals to you.

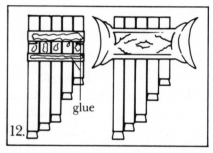

12. Put glue over the taped-together tubes as shown. Then lay the case-front, bird side up, over the glue. Press down and let dry.

13. Turn pipes over and glue the case-back on in the same way.

How to play:

Your panpipe is ready to be played. This is difficult to do, so don't get discouraged if you get no sound the first few tries.

Place the open end of tube #1 against the bottom of your lower lip. Blow across the top by whispering "too" as you blow. Make your lips very tight and thin, in a half smile. (This is just like blowing into a soda bottle.) Move the pipe higher or lower against your lip if the sound doesn't come out at first, and keep blowing and whispering "too" until you hear a note.

Play all the tubes from #1 to #5 and you will be playing the Japanese and Chinese pentatonic (5-note) scale.

Ancient songs:

No one knows exactly how these Chinese songs were played. See how many ways you can play them on your panpipe—try them fast, slow, soft, and loud. The numbers stand for the numbers of the tubes. (−) means rest for 1 beat. The slashes (/) divide the music into phrases.

Chinese Hymn

1234 / 544 − / 1234 / 544 − / 332 − /
332 − / 1234 / 541 − /

Chinese Melody

14 / 31 / 34 / 54 / 54 / 32 / 42 / 51 /
15 / 43 / 15 / 54 / 54 / 32 / 54 / 31 /

Compose your own songs and play them on your panpipe. Play a lively song. Play a sad song. Happy piping!

Cottage Maze

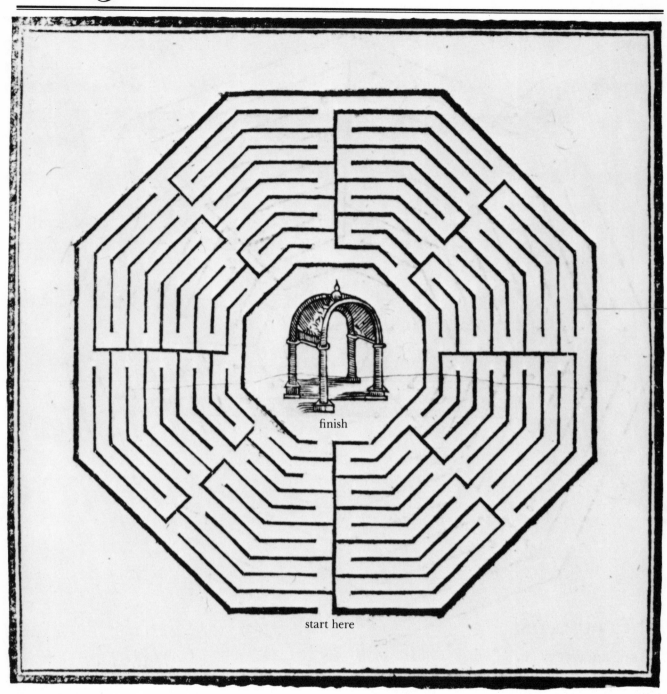

From a French book of garden designs by Daniel Loris, published in 1629.

Nine Men's Morris

The first known Nine Men's Morris game board was found carved into the roof of an Egyptian temple built in 1400 B.C.E., making it one of the oldest board games in the world. Ancient Morris boards have been found all over the world—from a board carved into stone steps in Sri Lanka in the first century, to part of a board found in a Norwegian Viking ship from about the tenth century, to boards from England, Iceland, Russia, Germany, and Czechoslovakia.

The design of the board appears in a book of magical formulas from Sri Lanka. Scholars think that people in ancient times believed that whoever won the game would have good luck. If you play and win the game, you too may have good luck!

The Nine Men's Morris board in the museum's collection is from a leather box that had three board games in it: a checkerboard, a backgammon board, and a Nine Men's Morris board. This wonderful box of games was made in Spain in the nineteenth century.

You will need:

scissors   corrugated cardboard
pencil   rubber cement
2 sets of 9 markers each—you can use buttons, coins, large pebbles, pieces of colored paper. The 2 sets should be different from each other.

What to do:

1. Tear out page 82 along perforations. Then cut out Morris board along outline.

2. Trace outline of the board onto cardboard and cut out cardboard square.

3. Glue or dry mount Morris board to the cardboard (see p. vii).

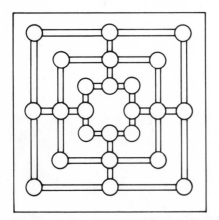

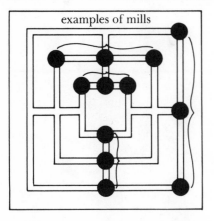

examples of mills

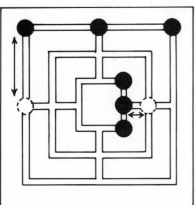

How to play:

This game is for 2 players. Each player has 9 markers of one color or shape. Markers may be placed on the corner of any square or where lines cross as shown.

    Flip a coin or draw straws to see who goes first.

1. Players take turns putting one marker at a time on any of the 24 points.

2. The object of the game is to place 3 markers in a row along any straight line on the board. These groups of 3 are called mills. When a player forms a mill, he can remove one of his opponent's markers. Markers in a mill, though, cannot be removed. Once a marker has been removed from the board, it is out of the game. When all the markers have been placed on the board, the second half of the game begins.

    On a player's turn, he must move only one of his markers one point in any direction along a straight line, trying to form a mill. Mills can be made, broken, and remade by moving markers back and forth on a straight line. Each time a player remakes a mill, he can remove his opponent's marker from the board. At the end of the game, if a player has only 3 markers left on the board and they are in a mill, he must break the mill when it is his turn.

3. To win the game, a player must reduce his opponent's markers to 2 pieces *or* he must block his opponent's markers so they cannot move in any direction.

Morse Code

Before the telegraph was invented, messages were sent by horseback, stagecoach, train, or boat. They took weeks or months to arrive (and sometimes never arrived at all!).

Samuel Finley Breese Morse changed all that. He invented the telegraph in 1835 and soon afterward invented the Morse code. The code is made up of dots and dashes that stand for every letter of the alphabet, every number, and even periods and commas. The telegraphs were connected by electrical wires (as telephones are). Someone tapped out short sounds (dots) and long sounds (dashes) on a metal bar on a sending machine. This sent short and long electrical impulses through the wires. The machine on the other end of the wires then received and delivered the message by tapping out those same long and short sounds. When the first telegraph cables were laid in 1838, it was the first time in history that people could communicate with each other quickly over great distances.

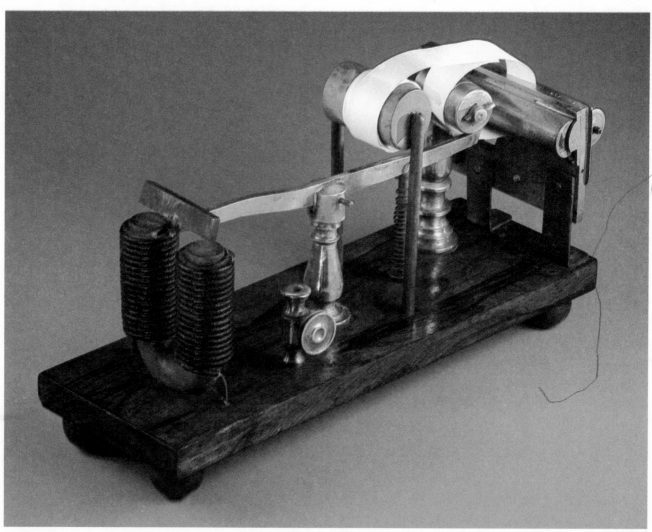

A model of one of Morse's first receiving telegraphs.

What to do:

Use the code below to send secret messages to a friend.

A •—	J •———	S •••	0 —————
B —•••	K —•—	T —	1 •————
C —•—•	L •—••	U ••—	2 ••———
D —••	M ——	V •••—	3 •••——
E •	N —•	W •——	4 ••••—
F ••—•	O ———	X —••—	5 •••••
G ——•	P •——•	Y —•——	6 —••••
H ••••	Q ——•—	Z ——••	7 ——•••
I ••	R •—•		8 ———••
			9 ————•

period •—•—•—
comma ——••——
colon ———•••
question mark ••——••
apostrophe •————•
quotation marks •—••—•

Messages to decipher:

Test your wits by decoding these riddles. | stands for the space between letters, || for the space between words. The answers are on page 87.

What did one unicorn say to the other?

—•——|———|••—||•—|•—•|•||•••|••••|•—|•—•|•——•||•—•—•—

Where do mummies go swimming?

••|—•||—|••••|•|••||—••|•|•—|—••||•••|•|•—||•—•—•—

Why did the mother camel call her baby Humphrey?

—•••|•|—•—•|•—|••—|•••|•||••••|•||••••|•—|—••||—•|———||••••|
••—|——|•——•|•—•—•—

On what kind of paper do mummies write?

•••|•—|—•|—••|•——•|•—|•——•|•|•—•|•—•—•—

Where did Michelangelo paint the Sistine Chapel?

•—••|—•——|••|—•|———•||———|—•||••••|••|•••||—•••|•—|—•—•|
—•—||•—•—•—

Why did the rooster on the weather vane refuse to fight?

••••|•||•——|•—|•••||—•—•|••••|••|—•—•|—•—|•|—•||•—•—•—

Why do mummies make good detectives?

—|••••|•|—•—||•——••|••|—•—|•||—|———||••—|—•|•—•|•—|•••—|
•|•—••||—|••••|•••|—•——•|•••||•—•—•—

85

Answers

Crammed into a Camel

17 people, 10 rabbits, 5 lions, 1 bird, 1 monkey, 1 dragon

Birds Galore

Perplexing Paths

Unicorn Tapestry Word Find

```
G P A K F H C M
U—N—I—C—O—R—N  C
T O B D U N A S
I I—L Q N S O T
B F F V T U J A
B R D L A U O G
A I E S I T E L
Q S—E—G—N—A—R—O
```

86

Harvester Word Find

```
T  E—H—T—Y—C—S  A
E  S  G  L  W  H  G  Q
K  G  R  F  K  U  S  J
S  B  A  T  J  R  D  B
A  C  N  E  O  C  R  P
C  U  N  V  H  H  I  E
H  I  A  M  E  W  B  D
W  Z  R—E—D—D—A—L
```

Marine Life Word Find

```
K  S—I—F  X  N  S  L
H  E—E—L  H  C  L  I
O  A  G  M  R  E  R  A
I  H  R  A  H  L  B  N
L—O—B—S—T—E—R—S
A—W—E—S—H  A  U  E
E  E  I—F—R  Q  T  S
S  E  D  B  L  R  I  F
```

Versailles Redesigned

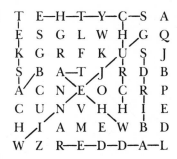

Cottage Maze

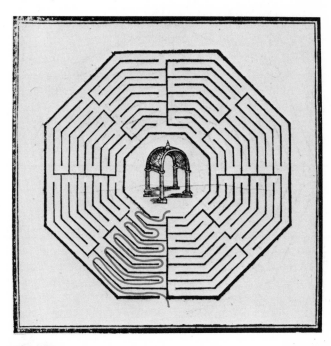

Three Heads Are Better Than One

Morse Code

You are sharp.
In the Dead Sea.
Because he had no hump (hump-free).
Sandpaper.
Lying on his back.
He was chicken.
They like to unravel things.

About the Author

Osa Brown made her first dollhouse (complete with working elevator) from boxes and scraps when she was seven years old. A few years later, when she completed a two-story model of an art museum with revolving doors and several exhibition halls, she knew she would pursue a career that combined crafts and the fine arts.

After graduating from the State University of New York at Stony Brook, Osa Brown got her Master's degree from the Bank Street College of Education in New York. She studied ceramics and art history in Italy and taught music and art in museums and schools in England and the United States. She now works at the Metropolitan Museum, where she develops and produces art-related books and materials.

Photograph Credits

Grateful acknowledgment is made for permission to reprint photographs of the following items from the Metropolitan's permanent collection: p. 1, Henry L. Phillips Collection, Bequest of Henry L. Phillips, 1939 (JP2795); p. 3, Bequest of Mrs. H. O. Havemeyer, 1929, H. O. Havemeyer Collection (JP1899); pp. 6–7, Gift of Lydia Bond Powel, 1951 (51.556.2); p. 8 (top), Gift of Lincoln Kirstein, 1952 (52.546.17); p. 8 (bottom), Pfeiffer Fund, 1962 (62.14); p. 11, The Elisha Whittelsey Collection, The Elisha Whittelsey Fund, 1962 (62.650.436); p. 13, The Elisha Whittelsey Collection, The Elisha Whittelsey Fund, 1962 (62.650.434); p. 15, The Harry G. C. Packard Collection of Asian Art, Gift of Harry G. C. Packard and Purchase, Fletcher, Rogers, Harris Brisbane Dick and Louis V. Bell Funds, Joseph Pulitzer Bequest and The Annenberg Fund, Inc., Gift, 1975 (1975.268.149); p. 16, Lent by Dr. and Mrs. Hiroshi Ueno, 1982 (Loan #1982.80); p. 17 (left), The Jefferson R. Burdick Collection, Gift of Jefferson R. Burdick (B27.14); p. 17 (right), The Jefferson R. Burdick Collection, Gift of Jefferson R. Burdick (25); p. 19, The Jefferson R. Burdick Collection, Gift of Jefferson R. Burdick (B31.3); p. 20, Gift of George D. Pratt, 1925 (25.83.6); p. 22 (left), Gift of Cele H. and William B. Rubin, 1961 (61.221 a-f); p. 22 (right), Harris Brisbane Dick Fund, 1939 (39.121); p. 23 (upper left), The Lesley and Emma Sheafer Collection, Bequest of Emma A. Sheafer, 1973 (1974.356.237 a, b); p. 23 (right), Gift of Dr. and Mrs. Brooks H. Marsh, 1976 (1976.341); p. 23 (lower left), The Crosby Brown Collection of Musical Instruments, 1889 (89.4.2418); p. 25, Gift of Mr. and Mrs. Henry Sherman, 1967 (67.260.5); p. 26, Purchase, 1930, The Cloisters Collection, 1930 (30.113.5); p. 29, Gift of Mrs. Otto Heinigke, 1916 (16.153.1); p. 30, The Cloisters Collection, Gift of John D. Rockefeller, Jr., 1937 (37.80.2); p. 31 (top), Anonymous Gift, 1930 (30.7.3); p. 31 (bottom), Purchase, Edward C. Moore, Jr., Gift, 1969 (69.135); p. 35, Purchase, 1960, Seymour Fund, 1960 (1960.1); p. 37, Rogers Fund, 1897; p. 38, Harris Brisbane Dick Fund, 1946; pp. 39, 41, 42, Gift of Lincoln Kirstein, 1970 (1970.565.450); pp. 43, 60, plates VI, VIII, Harris Brisbane Dick Fund, 1934 (34.78.1); pp. 44, 45, 47, Gift of Lincoln Kirstein, 1960 (JP3381); p. 48; Given to the United States by Egypt in 1965, awarded to The Metropolitan Museum of Art in 1967 and installed in The Sackler Wing in 1978; p. 59, Rogers Fund, 1919 (19.164); p. 61, Gift of J. Pierpont Morgan, 1917 (17.194.233); p. 64, "Portrait of a Young Man," Bequest of Mrs. H. O. Havemeyer, 1929, H. O. Havemeyer Collection (29.100.16); p. 65, Rogers Fund, 1904 (04.4.2); pp. 66–67, Bequest of Adele S. Colgate, 1962 (63.550.159); p. 68 (left), The Michael C. Rockefeller Memorial Collection, Purchase, Nelson A. Rockefeller Gift, 1964 (1978.412.109); p. 68 (right), The Michael C. Rockefeller Memorial Collection, Gift of Nelson A. Rockefeller, 1969 (1978.412.329); p. 69, The Michael C. Rockefeller Memorial Collection, Gift of Nelson A. Rockefeller, 1964 (1978.412.489); pp. 70–71, Gift and Bequest of Alice K. Bache, 1974, 1977 (1974.271.35); pp. 72, 73, Gift of Lincoln Kirstein, 1968 (69.503.11); p. 76, Gift of Mr. and Mrs. Erving Wolf, 1977 (1977.181); p. 77, The Crosby Brown Collection of Musical Instruments, 1889 (89.4.1547); p. 80, Daniel Loris, *Le Thresor des Parterres*, p. 198, Harris Brisbane Dick Fund, 1927 (27.66.1); pp. 81, 82, Gift of Gustavus A. Pfeiffer, 1948 (48.174.49); p. 84, Gift of George Hutchins, 1876 (76.7).